This book belongs to:

....

For my family
PB

This paperback edition first published in 2025 by Andersen Press Ltd.
First published in Great Britain in 2024 by Andersen Press Ltd.,
6 Coptic Street, London, WC1A 1NH, UK.
Vijverlaan 48, 3062 HL Rotterdam, Nederland.
Text copyright © Peter Bently 2024. Illustration copyright © Tor Freeman 2024.
The rights of Peter Bently and Tor Freeman to be identified as the author and illustrator of this work have been
asserted by them in accordance with the Copyright, Designs and Patents Act, 1988.
All rights reserved. Printed and bound in China.
1 3 5 7 9 10 8 6 4 2
British Library Cataloguing in Publication Data available. ISBN 978 1 83913 182 0

DOGDUNNIT

PETER BENTLY TOR FREEMAN

Andersen Press

Inspector Keyhole wore a frown.
A night of crime had swept the town.

Who chewed the rug?

Who trashed the chair?

Who scattered rubbish everywhere?

Tore Katie's favourite jeans to shreds?

Left muddy paw prints on the beds?

Who blocked the loo with Grandad's slippers?

Who scoffed the sausages and kippers?

Who sent a vase of flowers flying –
just where Mummy's phone was lying?

And who did a doo-doo,
small and neat,
that Daddy stood on –
in bare feet?

The great detective **Purrlock Jones**
Said, "I feel it in my bones.
It's **MOGGIARTY's** work, it's plain.
The **King of Crime** has struck again!"

Inspector Keyhole shook his head.
"It's **DOGS** what's done these crimes," he said.
"**It wasn't us!**" the dogs protested –

But **Keyhole** had them all arrested.

Purrlock watched and made a vow:
"I'll prove that **Keyhole's** wrong – but how?
Aha!" she said. "What's this I've found?
A **mouse's paw prints** on the ground!"

Soon the **dogs** all stood, dismayed,
Wearing **paw-cuffs** on parade.

Big and **small**
and **long** and **short**
Were led before the judge in court.

His Honour **Mister Justice Mogg**
Looked down severely at each dog.

"**You're guilty!**

It's as plain as day.

Lock these **CRIMINALS** away!"

Then **Purrlock Jones** burst into sight,
Crying, "**STOP!**" with all her might.
She said, "This mouse knows who's to blame!
Nibbler Watson is her name."

"Every night," declared the mouse,
"I like to **ramble** through each house
To check in all the floorboard cracks
For crumbs of **cheese** and other **snacks**.

Last night I saw a **rascal creeping**
While the dogs were soundly **sleeping**!
Everybody take a look
At these **videos** I took."

All the pooches started **growling**
When they watched the villain **prowling** –

And tearing **Katie's jeans** to shreds!
Leaving **paw prints** on the beds!
Stealing sausages and kippers!
Blocking up the loo with **slippers!**

Scattering sacks of stinky trash!
Sending vases flying – **SMASH!**

The dogs went wild. "**We told you so!** We're **innocent!** Please **let us go!!**"

The judge cried, "**No!** These films are **fake**. The dogs are **guilty**, no mistake!"

But **Purrlock** said, "There's one last scene. **Everybody watch the screen!**"

The mouse went on, "The **night** was **dark**.
I tracked that **baddie** through the **park** . . .

And saw him **slip in** through a flap,
Remove his mask, and take **a nap**."

"Good grief!" cried **Keyhole**. "I was wrong. It was **MOGGIARTY** all along!"

"Thanks," said **Purrlock** with a bow. "But where is **MOGGIARTY** now? That cunning **master of disguise**, Is **right** before our very **eyes**!

Who wants to **lock** up **every dog**? Who else but –

"Mister Justice MOGG!"

The culprit cried,

"You can't catch me!"

He tried to **flee**, but didn't see
The **mouse's tail**,
which made him **trip**,
**Stumble, tumble,
slide** and **slip**

Into the **arms** of **Sergeant Dawes**,

Who boomed, "**You're nicked!**" to great applause.

"**Well done, Watson!**" **Purrlock** cried.
"**Don't mention it!**" the mouse replied.

As the crook was led away
He hissed, "I'll be revenged one day!
Though **Purrlock Jones** has won this time
No jail can hold the **King of Crime**,

And as white is white and black is black –
MOGGIARTY will be back!"

The End

Other books written by Peter Bently

PANTemonium!

Skunk! Skedaddle!

The Great Dog Bottom Swap

The Great Sheep Shenanigans

The Great Balloon Hullaballoo

More books illustrated by Tor Freeman

Ten Fat Sausages

Bricks: The House a Greedy Pig Built

Find out more at www.andersenpress.co.uk